What Is a Green Roof?

By Vicki Sando

Illustrated by Zee Lehar

NAUSICAA
VALLEY PRESS

Vicki Sando is a NYC public school teacher and educational green roof advocate.
vickisando.com

Zee Lehar is a professional illustrator and graphic designer.
instagram.com/moon_milkk

Copy Editor: Jane Lerner

Nausicaa Valley Press
nausicaavalleypress.org
Copyright ©2020 Nausicaa Valley Press
Vicki Sando & Zee Lehar

Library of Congress Cataloging-in-Publication Data
Sando, Vicki
What Is a Green Roof? / by Vicki Sando; Illustrated by Zee Lehar

Library of Congress Control Number: 2020930781

ISBN 978-1-7341672-0-7

To Kelly Shannon, my mentor and friend.
-VS

Thanks to my artistic mother, Cecilia, for inspiring my creativity, and to my father Alan for supporting my art education.
-ZL

A bird's-eye view of New York City reveals many types of rooftops: black, silver, stone, blue, and green.

Blue

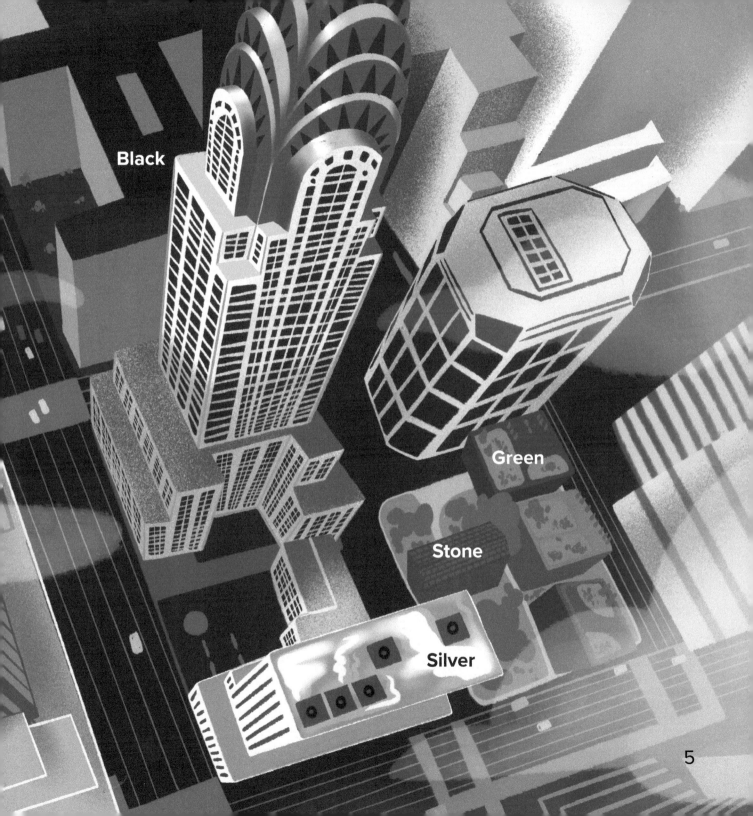

5

Some roofs are made
of black tar to absorb
the sun's heat.

Some roofs are painted
silver to help reflect
the sun's rays.

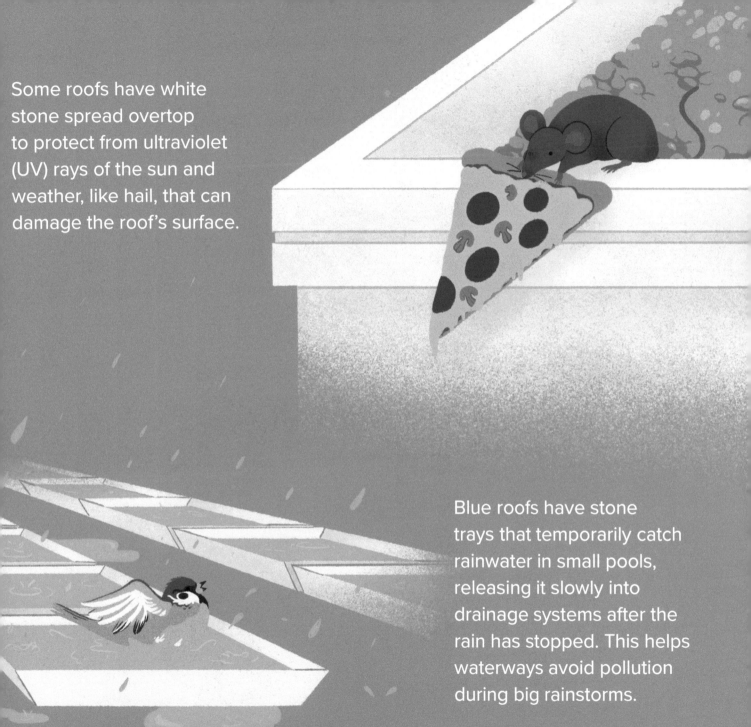

Some roofs have white stone spread overtop to protect from ultraviolet (UV) rays of the sun and weather, like hail, that can damage the roof's surface.

Blue roofs have stone trays that temporarily catch rainwater in small pools, releasing it slowly into drainage systems after the rain has stopped. This helps waterways avoid pollution during big rainstorms.

7

And some are **green roofs,** also known as "vegetated roofs" or "living roofs." These are rooftops covered with layers of plant root barriers, water drainage systems, **growing media** (soil), and plants on top of a roof surface.

Unlike other rooftops, green roofs are made of different layers to protect the bottom roof surface from root damage, help plants grow, and let water flow slowly off the roof and into drainage systems.

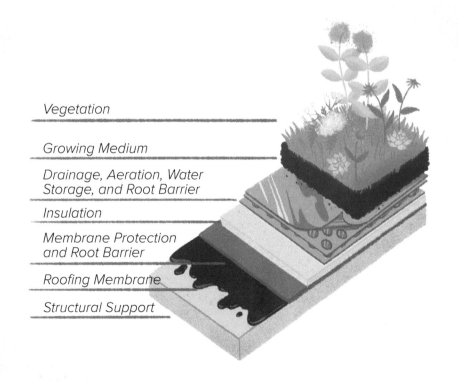

Vegetation

Growing Medium

Drainage, Aeration, Water Storage, and Root Barrier

Insulation

Membrane Protection and Root Barrier

Roofing Membrane

Structural Support

People began building green roofs centuries ago.

The Hanging Gardens of Babylon (built in 630 BCE in present-day Iraq) is one of the Seven Wonders of the Ancient World. Trees and plants were watered by aqueducts, a series of channels that carried water along the building's rooftops.

Over 1,000 years ago, Vikings from Scandinavia built green roofs. Their homes were made of an inner frame of wood covered with a thick layer of soil and plants, making these houses very sturdy, compared to plain wooden structures. The green roof also kept the homes warmer in the winter and cooler in the summer.

Today, there are two main types of green roofs: **extensive** and **intensive**.

An **extensive** green roof is less than 6 inches (15.24 cm) in depth and planted with sedums and low-growing native plants.

The Jacob Javits Center has the largest green roof in New York City.

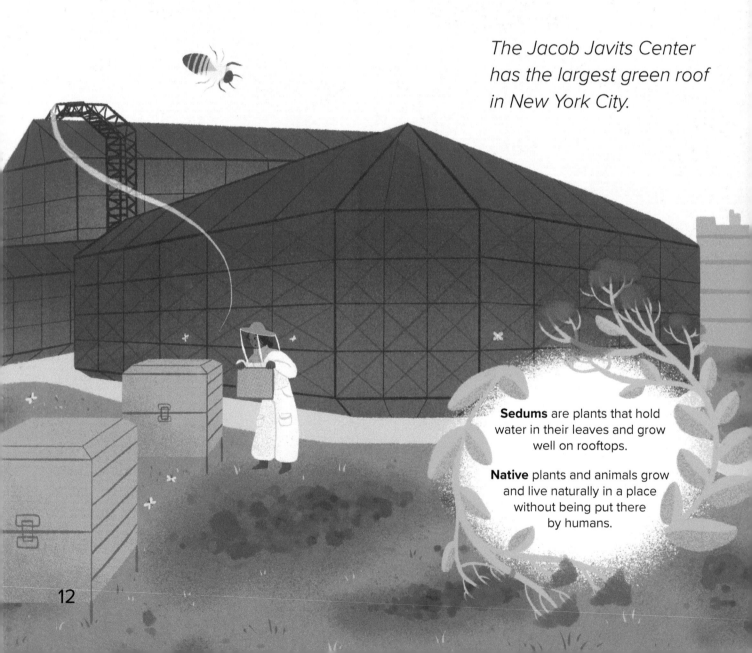

Sedums are plants that hold water in their leaves and grow well on rooftops.

Native plants and animals grow and live naturally in a place without being put there by humans.

An **intensive** green roof is greater than 6 inches in depth and can support larger plants and trees.

The High Line, an elevated former railroad line from the 1930s, is now a 1.45-mile-long stretch (2.3 km) of greenway planted with over 500 species of plants and trees.

13

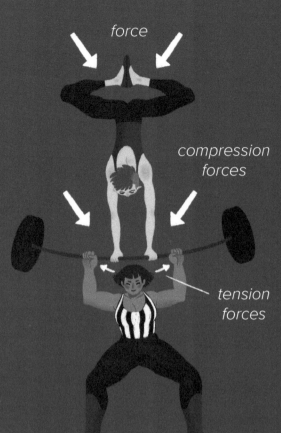

force

compression forces

tension forces

Before installing a green roof, a structural engineer must first evaluate the frame or skeleton of a building to determine how much extra weight or load a building can support.

dead load

live load

Weight or **load** on a structure causes **compression** (a pushing force) or **tension** (a pulling force). There are two main types of load: **live load**, which is anything moving across a surface, or **dead load**, which is a non-movable weight on a roof.

14

Green roofs help our environment in many ways.

Green roofs reduce **stormwater runoff;** when it rains, they are like sponges and absorb water, releasing it slowly down drainage systems. In cities with a combined sewer system — meaning underground wastewater pipes carry both sewage and stormwater — a heavy rainstorm can flood the system, sending untreated sewage into rivers, streams, and lakes.

15

Green roofs are like a blanket and keep buildings cooler in the summer and warmer in the winter, saving energy. Plants also release water vapor from their leaves, thereby cooling the surrounding environment. Green roofs also help reduce urban **heat island effect**, which is caused by cities having hotter temperatures than surrounding areas because buildings, roadways, and cars absorb and produce heat energy.

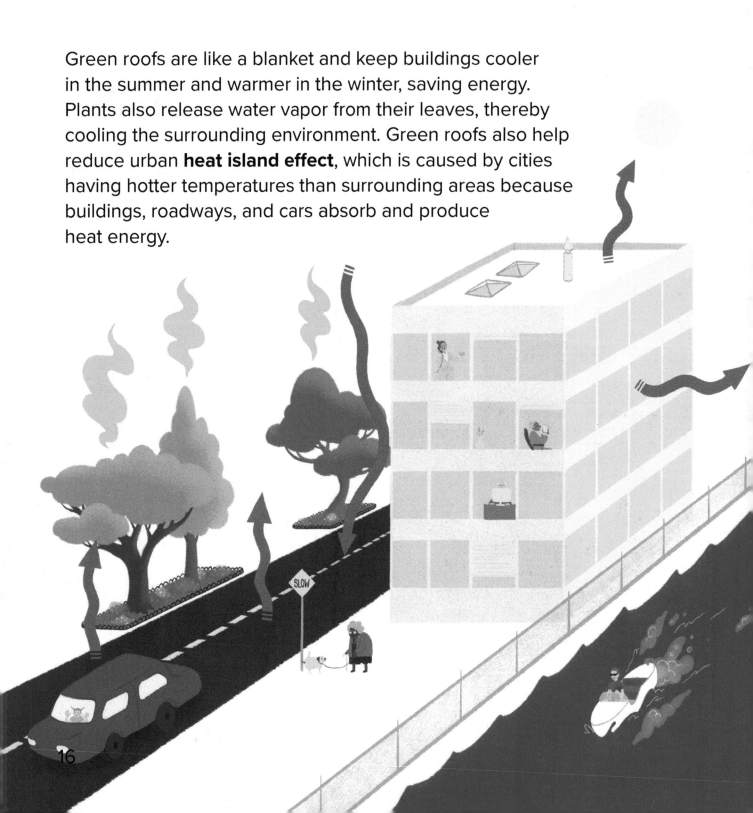

SLOW

Green roofs are also wildlife **habitats,** which is important in cities where there are fewer trees and plants for insects and birds. People also need green space in urban areas for their health and wellbeing.

Kingsland Wildflowers green roof is in an industrial area in Greenpoint, Brooklyn. Scientists have observed dozens of native and migrating birds, bats, and insect species on the several rooftops it covers.

A habitat is a place where wildlife can find food, water, shelter, and mates.

17

Green roofs can link parks and other green spaces together to create wildlife pathways across cities for native and migrating birds and insects.

Green roofs can be found on many types of structures.

Entertainment Centers: Barclays Center Brooklyn, NYC

The green roof plants absorb sound coming from inside the building.

Post Offices: The NY Morgan Mail Processing Center, NYC

This is the USPS's first green roof in the country.

Office Buildings: Midtown Sky Garden, NYC

Scientific studies have proven that people work and feel better when they look at nature.

Houses and Apartment Buildings: Battery Park City, NYC

People prefer to live near green space.

Empire State Building: NYC

There are even four green roofs on the Empire State Building!

School Buildings: PS 41, NYC

Green roofs on schools help children get outside and learn in nature while reducing the building's energy use.

Green roofs can also be used to grow food in urban environments.

Brooklyn Grange: Brooklyn and Queens, NYC

They operate the world's largest rooftop farms on two roofs in Brooklyn and Queens, in New York City.

Restaurants: Rosemary's West Village, NYC

The chef grows fresh vegetables and herbs for the restaurant's menu.

"Living walls" are another way to green buildings. Plants are grown on the side of a structure using a grid system. Living walls can offer some of the same benefits that green roofs provide on roof tops.

This living wall is located at 685 Third Avenue in NYC.

If more rooftops around the world were covered with green roofs, we could save energy, have cooler temperatures in cities, cleaner water, and grow food closer to consumers. By adding more green space, we help wildlife and have a healthier and more beautiful environment.

When individuals take the time to make a difference to our environment, the effect is more significant than we might think!

Glossary

Compression - A squeezing force that makes something smaller.

Critical load - The maximum weight a structure can support before breaking.

Dead load - Any nonmoving weight on a structure.

Extensive green roof - A vegetative roof 6 inches (15.24 cm) or less in depth and planted with sedums and/or native plants.

Green roof - A roof surface mostly covered with vegetation, growing media (soil), and other layers that protect the roof surface.

Growing Media - Special lightweight soil that drains water well.

Habitat - A place where wildlife can find food, water, shelter, and mates.

Heat island effect - When cities have hotter temperatures than surrounding areas because buildings, roadways, and cars absorb and produce heat energy.

Intensive green roof - A vegetative roof deeper than 6 inches (15.24 cm) that can support large plants, such as tall grasses, shrubs, and trees.

Live load - Any weight on a structure that is moving, such as people walking or cars driving.

Native - A plant or animal that grows and lives in a place without having been introduced by humans.

Stormwater runoff - When rainwater is not absorbed by the ground surface and flows into waterways, often carrying pollution.

Structural load - A weight or force added to a structure.

Tension - A pulling force that stretches something tighter.

For further green roof information and curriculum visit:
educationalgreenroofs.org
greenroofsnyc.com
greenroofs.org

CPSIA information can be obtained
at www.ICGtesting.com
Printed in the USA
BVHW021954181220
596020BV00009B/17